# 501 EXCUSES

## — FOR A BAD —

# GOLF SHOT

JUSTIN J. EXNER

Published by Sourcebooks, Inc.
P.O. Box 4410, Naperville, Illinois 60567-4410
(630) 961-3900
Fax: (630) 961-2168
sourcebooks.com

Printed and bound in China.
LEO 20 19 18 17 16 15 14 13 12 11

I dedicate this book to my family,
with special thanks to my mother Janet.
I love you all.

In addition, I'd like to thank all those
who believed in me, and especially those who did not.

# There is no excuse
# for a bad golf shot, but...

## • 1 •

A drop of sweat fell in my eye and I missed the ball.

## • 2 •

I stubbed my toe on the base of my bed,
now I can't wear my golf shoes.

## • 3 •

I've only played with these clubs twice.

## • 4 •

My rain suit is too tight
and I can't swing my club smoothly.

## • 5 •

My ball is all scuffed up.

## • 6 •

I keep picking up my head. I'm afraid the geese
are going to do their business on me.

## • 7 •

The tee was leaning too far forward.

## • 8 •

I get nervous hitting last all the time.

## • 9 •

The sun was in my eyes.

## • 10 •

I have tendonitis in my left foot.

## • 11 •

My dog chewed up my golf glove.

## • 12 •

I just took a lesson and I can't get used
to my new setup and grip.

### • 13 •

I hit it off the heel of the club.

### • 14 •

My clubs need to be re-gripped.
They keep slipping out of my hand.

### • 15 •

I'm missing some spikes on my golf shoes
and it makes me slip.

### • 16 •

I thought you said, "Dogleg left."

### • 17 •

I thought this was the 9-iron, not the 6.

### • 18 •

The golfers on the other tee box were talking
and I couldn't concentrate.

### • 19 •

The greens are a lot faster than they look.

### • 20 •

These new shoes are killing me.
I think I'll get a cart for the back nine.

### • 21 •

It's this new putter.

### • 22 •

The ball washer was out of water.
I couldn't focus with that speck of dirt on the ball.

### • 23 •

Did you see that? A bug landed on my ball
just as I was starting my downswing!

### • 24 •

The wind was with me when I was lining up the shot.

**· 25 ·**

I thought we were using the green over *there*.

## • 26 •

It's my first time out this year.

## • 27 •

This is my first time out since my bypass operation.

## • 28 •

I left my sunglasses in my other golf bag.

## • 29 •

*These* are my wife's clubs.
Mine are being re-gripped.

## • 30 •

It must have kicked the wrong way off the hill,
because the shot looked perfect.

## • 31 •

I didn't follow through on the swing.

## • 32 •

It's just too hot to be playing golf.

## • 33 •

It's just too cold to be playing golf.

## • 34 •

My ball isn't white.
I can only play with white golf balls.


## • 35 •

This ball is white.
I only play well when I use pink golf balls.


## • 36 •

I've run out of white tees.
I only play well with white tees.


## • 37 •

My caddy gave me the wrong club.

## • 38 •

My knee hurts from an old high school football injury.

## • 39 •

I didn't follow through with my hips.

## • 40 •

I'm doing exactly what my golf instructor told me to do, but the ball keeps slicing.

## • 41 •

A pebble deflected my putt to the left.

# 42

I can't remember
if I'm supposed to inhale
or exhale on impact.

### • 43 •

I focus my attention on putting, not on my drives.

### • 44 •

I took too much of the earth on that swing.

### • 45 •

The greenkeeper usually double cuts the greens,
but he obviously didn't today.
These greens are way too slow.

### • 46 •

That was supposed to be a practice swing.

### • 47 •

I just didn't get all of the ball.

### • 48 •

My dog urinated on my good golf shoes
so I have to play in my sneakers.

### • 49 •

There's a nick on my ball, so it spun out of bounds.

### • 50 •

Boy, the greenkeeper must be in an awful mood. I've
never seen so many tough pin positions.

## • 51 •

I play better with golfers
who are actually good.

## • 52 •

These are new clubs.

## • 53 •

There's too much sand in these bunkers.

## • 54 •

I had too big a breakfast.
I can't get the club around my gut.

## • 55 •

I didn't have time to warm up.
I usually hit a bucket of balls before playing.

## • 56 •

The airline lost my clubs—again. I'm using rentals.

## • 57 •

Those hedges were just planted.
That's a do-over.

## • 58 •

My socks are wet from the rain.
I keep slipping in my shoes.

## • 59 •

The group ahead of us is playing too slow.
It's throwing off my rhythm.

## • 60 •

I can't play on this course.
I haven't been able to practice it on virtual golf.

## • 61 •

It's impossible to get a true roll on these greens—no one
repairs their ball marks here.

## • 62 •

I hit it off the toe of the club.

## • 63 •

I left my lucky visor in the car.

## • 64 •

I lost one of my contacts and the flagstick is all fuzzy.

## • 65 •

This course does not have the yardage marked accurately.
There is no way that was 139 yards.

## • 66 •

I must be allergic to the pesticide spray.
My eyes keep watering and I can't see the ball.

## • 67 •

Taking a cart throws my timing off.
I usually visualize my next shot
as I am walking up to the ball.

## • 68 •

It must have been that last beer.
I had a great round going.

## • 69 •

I couldn't see from back there that
it was not a vertical water hazard.

## • 70 •

The putting green was closed this morning.

### • 71 •

Since canceling my subscription to *Golf Digest*,
I just don't play well.

### • 72 •

I was thrown out of my Tuesday evening group for slow
play, so I haven't been able to get out regularly.

### • 73 •

I didn't have lunch.
I have no energy.

### • 74 •

If the pin was pulled, it would have gone in.

## 75

I quit smoking yesterday.

### • 76 •

My neck is stiff; I must have slept on it wrong.

### • 77 •

I didn't know it was against the rules
to tell a competitor what club I used.

### • 78 •

I thought you get a mulligan every hole.
That's the way I was taught.

### • 79 •

The slope on that green is subtle but severe.

## • 80 •

I've been working on my MBA.
I just haven't had time to practice.

## • 81 •

The ground is too dry.
My divots aren't coming off smoothly.

## • 82 •

My golf glove is wet.
I can't get a grip on the club.

## • 83 •

The driving range uses a different type of golf ball.
I can't seem to gauge my distance.

### • 84 •

I'm too busy at work to get away and play.
I'm inconsistent.

### • 85 •

My wife won't let me play since having the kid.
I knew I should have gotten a dog instead.

### • 86 •

The driving range was closed.

### • 87 •

I'm having trouble adjusting to these left-handed
clubs—but I did save twenty dollars.

## • 88 •

The sunscreen I put on my hands
made them greasy and my club slipped.

## • 89 •

I'm still depressed from the eighteen holes yesterday.

## • 90 •

I have tennis elbow.
What the heck is tennis elbow anyway?

## • 91 •

My rain suit is at home.
I don't play well while wearing wet clothes.

## • 92 •

My wife is pregnant and I can't get any sleep.

## • 93 •

The nearest golf course is 200 miles from my house.

## • 94 •

That acorn threw off my putt.

## • 95 •

I've had to play softball
every Saturday and Sunday this summer.
I just haven't been out.

## • 96 •

I haven't had any money to play;
my school loans are due.

## • 97 •

I always get kicked off the course for being intoxicated.
This is the first round I've finished in over two years.

## • 98 •

My back is sunburned. It hurts to swing.

## • 99 •

I have a tear in my golf glove.

### • 100 •

I don't know why I bought clubs with graphite shafts.
Steel is the way to go.

### • 101 •

This course doesn't let you chip on the practice green.

### • 102 •

My short game is not what I focused on in my last lesson.

### • 103 •

I forgot to take my watch off
and it threw off my balance.

## • 104 •

My putting lesson was rained out last week.

## • 105 •

I ran out of tees, so I had to use half a tee
and I couldn't get the loft required to fly the trap.

## • 106 •

I cut my hand at work,
so I can't get a firm grip on the clubs.

## • 107 •

It rained all week and I couldn't practice.

# · 108 ·

Did you see that?
That bird deflected my shot
into the woods!

## • 109 •

I have a headache from the concert last night.
I just can't concentrate.

## • 110 •

I thought this was a par 5, not a 4!
I was laying up on my second shot.

## • 111 •

It was a tough week at work and I don't seem
to have any energy left for my golf game.

## • 112 •

I'm getting tired.
I usually take a cart.

## • 113 •

I have to accept that my swing speed
is decreasing now that I'm over fifty.

## • 114 •

You should have told me about the water on this hole.

## • 115 •

This is one of those courses you need to play a few times
before you can expect to score well.

## • 116 •

I don't have a sand wedge.
I lost it in the lake last time I played.

## • 117 •

I didn't open my stance and I pushed the ball to the left.

## • 118 •

I usually play from the championship tees.
Moving up confuses me.

## • 119 •

Someone stole my good clubs because
I forgot to set the alarm on my golf bag.

## • 120 •

I can't play my best when I have to wait between shots.
What's taking those guys so long?

## • 121 •

Those guys were making too much noise
on the other fairway.

## • 122 •

My shoes aren't tied tightly enough.

## • 123 •

I moved my body too far forward on impact and sliced
it into the fairway, but it rolled into the woods.

## • 124 •

The greens are much faster in Florida.

## • 125 •

I forgot my antacid and I have bad indigestion from eating so many Milk Duds while watching *Caddyshack* last night.

**· 126 ·**

This area wasn't considered
out-of-bounds last year.

### • 127 •

These greens have way too much sand on them.
It slows down all my putts.

### • 128 •

I didn't have oatmeal for breakfast—
I only play well when I eat oatmeal for breakfast.

### • 129 •

I can't keep my head still on the backswing.

### • 130 •

I have a bad case of jet lag.

### • 131 •

My other driver has an 11.5-degree loft.
I can't hit a 9-degree driver.


### • 132 •

I didn't keep my left arm in.


### • 133 •

I gripped the club too far down and topped the ball.


### • 134 •

I just can't keep my mind off her; it's so frustrating.
Where is the beer girl anyway?

## • 135 •

I don't know what the hell is wrong.

## • 136 •

The ball should go left if the ball is above my feet.

## • 137 •

I pushed my hips too much
while trying to get out of that fairway trap.

## • 138 •

The ranger keeps following me around.
I can't focus when I'm being watched.

## • 139 •

I ate way too much on the turn; now I'm bloated.

## • 140 •

The hail keeps hitting my eyes.
Maybe we should wait until the storm passes.

## • 141 •

The balls fly much farther in Colorado.
I can't get my distance gauged.

## • 142 •

My wrists aren't breaking on impact.

· 143 ·

Do those ducks ever quit quacking? I can't believe how loud they are.

### • 144 •

I have a bad back from rugby practice yesterday.

### • 145 •

Those low-flying airplanes are really annoying.

### • 146 •

That bee must be addicted to my cologne.
It keeps following me from hole to hole.

### • 147 •

The fairway looks like it slopes to the left, not the right.

## • 148 •

My hands were too far to the left on my grip.

## • 149 •

I keep closing the club face
and I can't get the loft to clear the red tees.

## • 150 •

I can't get loose—my chiropractor is out of town.

## • 151 •

My grip just isn't comfortable.

### • 152 •

I've lost all my money gambling
and now I can't afford lessons.

### • 153 •

My wife was awarded my twenty-two backup putters
in the divorce settlement, and now I have to play
with this darn thing.

### • 154 •

I pulled a muscle in my leg while helping
an elderly lady get her bag out of her car trunk.

### • 155 •

I hurt my hips having sex last night.

## • 156 •

The sand trap should not be right
in the middle of the fairway.
Oh, I thought that was our fairway.

## • 157 •

I slept on my shoulder the wrong way.
Now my swing is all messed up.

## • 158 •

I wanted to practice, but the range was out of balls.

## • 159 •

I focus too much on where the ball is going.
I can never follow through.

## • 160 •

Those swing machines are too expensive.

## • 161 •

Damn it, have you no etiquette?
Please quit breathing when I swing.

## • 162 •

I duffed the shot. No excuse for that.

## • 163 •

I made it over the lake last time.
It must be the humidity.

### • 164 •

The sand is much heavier in Scotland.

### • 165 •

When I'm on the practice tee,
the ball always goes straight.

### • 166 •

I pulled the putter too far back.

### • 167 •

The instructor told me to play my slice
and now I hit the ball straight.

## • 168 •

I'm just not releasing on the ball.

## • 169 •

Didn't you hear that sound in the woods during my
swing? It sounded like a duck.

## • 170 •

My old caddy's notes are in Japanese
and I can't interpret them since he was deported.

## • 171 •

These balls don't fly as far as yours,
but I got a good deal on mine.

### • 172 •

I lined up with the ball too close to my left foot.

### • 173 •

The wind keeps shifting direction when I hit.

### • 174 •

I hurt my elbow when I got out of that damn cart.

### • 175 •

I just need to work on my grip.

### • 176 •

My swing looks perfect on video;
I don't know what's wrong.

### • 177 •

I just don't have any rhythm today.
I need to listen to some music.

### • 178 •

I forgot about that trap in front of the green.

### • 179 •

I am hitting the ball too perfectly.
It keeps going too far.

## • 180 •

I keep pulling the ball.
It must be the aerobics I've been taking.

## • 181 •

Damn it! Damn it! Damn it!

## • 182 •

I'm getting off the tee fine—
it's my short game that's so bad.

## • 183 •

When I yelled, "fore," my caddy
thought that was the club I needed.

• 184 •

I needed to use a seven,
not an eight, just short
of a hole in one.

## • 185 •

I play better with women.
They motivate me.

## • 186 •

I decided to become celibate yesterday.

## • 187 •

Someone left a cigar burning on the green
and it made my putt drift.

## • 188 •

I hate these soft spikes.
I keep slipping.

## • 189 •

I played the ball too far back in my stance
and I couldn't get it over that tree.

## • 190 •

I took too much sand on that swing.

## • 191 •

These balatas spin too much.
I like a harder-shelled ball.

## • 192 •

My backswing is way too short.

### • 193 •

I was up all night watching *M\*A\*S\*H* reruns.
I didn't get any rest.

### • 194 •

My arm moved too far to the left of the vertex.

### • 195 •

I always have trouble focusing on the ball
when the sun is setting.

### • 196 •

I always choke when money is on the line.

### • 197 •

I always aim too far left
when coming out of the bunker.

### • 198 •

My backswing is too flat.

### • 199 •

Rough should test you, not penalize you one stroke.
This is unfair.

### • 200 •

That Golf Channel has me all screwed up.

## • 201 •

The wind is chasing us.
It seems like we are always playing into the wind.

## • 202 •

I never follow through
when trying to get out of a bunker.

## • 203 •

Ever since I made a hole in one, I can't concentrate.

## • 204 •

I read way too much into the putts.

## • 205 •

I never had a shot—the tree was in the way.

## • 206 •

I just can't gauge the chip shots like I used to.

## • 207 •

I can't get my wedge to bite.

## • 208 •

My ball was buried in the middle of a footprint.
Some idiot didn't rake the trap.

### • 209 •

I've been going at the flagstick way too often.

### • 210 •

The practice green was much faster.

### • 211 •

I need to relax and take a deep breath.
I'm playing way too fast.

### • 212 •

I forgot my umbrella in the car.
Now my glasses are foggy.

## • 213 •
Fore!!!!!!!!

## • 214 •
I never saw the break from that angle.

## • 215 •
I lifted the tip of the putter too high off the ground.

## • 216 •
I have to go to the bathroom; I can't concentrate.

**· 217 ·**

You're never watching when
I hit a good shot.

### • 218 •

I never tilted my shoulders.

### • 219 •

My angle of impact exceeded the reflection angle,
causing me to duff the shot.

### • 220 •

When the hole was moved,
the greenkeeper left a gap in the green.
There goes my eagle.

### • 221 •

It's only the eighteenth hole.
I'm not quite warmed up yet.

### • 222 •

So what if it was a three-footer?
I was only trying to get the ball close, not make it.

### • 223 •

I knew I had a mulligan left!

### • 224 •

The weatherman said it was going to warm up.
I should have brought my sweater; I'm chilly.

### • 225 •

It's not my swing—it's these old clubs!

## • 226 •

I just can't generate the power
that I could when I was young.

## • 227 •

I'm sorry I'm playing so poorly.
My wife reminded me that I'm scheduled
for my annual checkup tomorrow.

## • 228 •

My boss is a jerk.
I can't relax.

## • 229 •

My dog chewed a hole in my good golf shoes.

## • 230 •

I usually walk.
This "riding in a cart" is not allowing me
to find my rhythm.

## • 231 •

I had a blind shot, but the ball went where I hit it.
I just didn't see the pond.

## • 232 •

My phone vibrated during that putt.

## • 233 •

I just want the most strokes for the money—
to heck with my score.

**234**

All the weight lifting
I'm doing has made me
too huge for golf.

## • 235 •

All the golf schools I liked were too expensive—
so I'm self-taught.

## • 236 •

I can't play in seventy-degree, sunny weather.
I need snow, wind, and rain.

## • 237 •

Tournament pressure is hard to handle.

## • 238 •

The slow play throws off my concentration.
It shouldn't take five and a half hours for a round.

## • 239 •

I only play well on hilly courses.

## • 240 •

You should have seen me play last week.

## • 241 •

I usually use titanium clubs.
These tungsten clubs are too light.

## • 242 •

The geese keep following me.
It makes me nervous.

## • 243 •

I had to lay up; I was just using the 3-wood
for the heck of it.

## • 244 •

My usual golf cart is electric.
This gas-powered one is uncomfortable and noisy.

## • 245 •

I never aligned the club face on my setup.

## • 246 •

I left my new clubs in my other car.

### • 247 •

My children don't count my whiff.

### • 248 •

My other driver is an 8.5-degree loft, not a 10-degree.
I'm losing too much distance out of the box.

### • 249 •

My ball was resting on a tree stump.

### • 250 •

I'm getting married in three hours—
it's hard to concentrate.

## • 251 •

The lessons I took on the Internet
are not working the way they said they would.

## • 252 •

My ball was wedged in the corner
between the grass and sand.
I had no shot.

## • 253 •

My country club's fairways are much better.
These conditions are unplayable.

## • 254 •

I had the club face opened too much in the bunker.

## • 255 •

My allergies are killing me.
I can't deal with all the pressure.

## • 256 •

My regular caddy was arrested. This guy is an idiot—
he doesn't know a 3-wood from a 5-wood.

## • 257 •

The lie I had wasn't perfectly perfect.

## • 258 •

I broke my pitching wedge the last time I played.
This sand wedge has too much loft.

## • 259 •

It's too humid.
My shirt is sticking to my body.

## • 260 •

The greens are too fast.
They are like ice.

## • 261 •

I can't play with these golf balls.
The numbers are too high.

## • 262 •

I thought if the ball is above your feet it will slice.

### • 263 •

My athlete's foot is causing me to mishit.

### • 264 •

The chipping area was closed at three a.m.
(that's when I came to practice).

### • 265 •

I just moved to a new house and my back is aching.
I have no follow-through.

### • 266 •

I play better with a hard golf ball.
These soft ones are for the pros.

### • 267 •

My clubs are too old.
These wooden shafts don't have the right flex.

### • 268 •

The ball was wedged up against the tree.
I had no shot.

### • 269 •

The greens I normally play on are much slower.

### • 270 •

The marshal told me to lay up on this hole.
I am a fool for listening.

### • 271 •

I keep moving my putter when I swing my shoulders.

### • 272 •

The grass bunker gave me no shot.
Who the hell designed this course?

### • 273 •

The carpet in my living room
doesn't break like this green.

### • 274 •

There is too much goose crap on the course.

## • 275 •
I keep second-guessing my shots.

## • 276 •
Your cigar smoke keeps getting in my eyes when I putt.

## • 277 •
The clubs I ordered on the Internet haven't arrived yet.
I'm stuck with these old ones.

## • 278 •
This copper bracelet is too tight on my wrist.
I can't hold on to the club.

## • 279 •

I never got comfortable over the ball.

## • 280 •

My ball ricocheted off that water pump
and went into the woods.
Shouldn't I get a do-over?

## • 281 •

I'm taking my club back too fast.

## • 282 •

The guy on the Golf Channel
hit these clubs perfectly every time.
They don't seem to work for me.

**· 283 ·**

To hell with the tournament.
I don't look good in a
green jacket anyway.

### • 284 •

My wife didn't wash my lucky golf shirt.

### • 285 •

I thought when I turned forty
I could play from the gold tees.

### • 286 •

I can't judge the distance of my ball
in this cool December air.

### • 287 •

My dog was sick last night.
I didn't get any sleep.

## • 288 •

I don't like this gripless putter,
but my broker gave it to me.

## • 289 •

My shirt is itchy.
I bet you my wife forgot to use the fabric softener again.

## • 290 •

Titanium balls fly too far for my ability.

## • 291 •

From three hundred yards out it looks like the green
slopes away. I should have laid up.

### • 292 •

The guys behind us are pushing us.
They are making me nervous.

### • 293 •

The snow keeps getting in my eyes.

### • 294 •

My pants are too tight—
but I think the beer girl likes them.

### • 295 •

There is no way this is a 500-yard hole—
it's only 490.

### • 296 •

I had a root canal last month.
It still hurts when I golf.

### • 297 •

I got whiplash when you started the cart.
Now my neck hurts.

### • 298 •

I had to take a drop.
The speed limit sign was in the way.

### • 299 •

I can't play well unless I'm clean shaven.

### • 300 •

I just can't find the sweet spot today.

### • 301 •

That putt should have gone in.
My ball must be lopsided.

### • 302 •

This green isn't fair. It's surrounded by bunkers.

### • 303 •

The rye grass isn't fair.
I can't play on anything but bluegrass.

### • 304 •

I only play well when I bet.

### • 305 •

I lost my contact lens on the last hole.
I'm playing one-eyed.

### • 306 •

I haven't refilled my medication this week.

### • 307 •

I must need new glasses.
I can't seem to read a putt today.

· 308 ·

I hate playing on Sundays.
They won't serve me beer
until 11:00 a.m.

## • 309 •

My ball must have hit a sprinkler head.
It ended up in the water.
I never go in the water.

## • 310 •

Did you see that? The head of my driver
flew off during my swing!

## • 311 •

That putt was short because I'm using those South
American golf balls. It was a whole revolution short.

## • 312 •

That car door slammed while I was swinging!

### • 313 •

I pulled the putt because an ant crawled on my shoe.

### • 314 •

I didn't have a 3-wood so I had to use my 5-wood.

### • 315 •

These are my wife's golf shoes.
Mine are being re-spiked.

### • 316 •

You were moving when I was attempting my birdie putt.

## • 317 •

I lost the ball in the fog,
but it was headed straight for the green.
Someone must have picked it up.

## • 318 •

My hands are sweaty and the clubhouse had no soap.

## • 319 •

The ball doesn't fly as far here as in Canada.

## • 320 •

I drank too much coffee—I have the shakes.

## • 321 •

When you leaned on your putter,
it left an indentation on the green.

## • 322 •

A bunch of hackers must have torn up the green.
I can't play competitively under these circumstances.

## • 323 •

My subscription to *Golf Digest* ran out this month.

## • 324 •

I was better before I retired.
I just don't have time to golf anymore.

### • 325 •

I would rather be home cleaning the basement than playing on this cow pasture they call a golf course.

### • 326 •

The cable went out at home last night,
and I missed my final lesson on the Golf Channel.

### • 327 •

My hat is too tight; it's giving me a headache.

### • 328 •

My lucky hat is in my wife's car.
Otherwise that putt would have dropped.

### • 329 •

I don't like these balls I bought over the Internet.
They fly too far.

### • 330 •

The bookstore was out of *Golf Magazine*.

### • 331 •

If the lip on the hole weren't pushed up,
it would have fallen in.

### • 332 •

I'm in the middle of a divorce.

### • 333 •

I can't tee off unless a crowd of people is watching.

### • 334 •

The airline ground crew cracked my driver.
Now I have to tee off with my 3-wood.

### • 335 •

This new ball I'm playing has much less spin than
my old one. I thought that shot would check up.

### • 336 •

The GPS on this cart is way off.

### • 337 •
That car dealership overcharged me
so I can't afford the good balls.

### • 338 •
I have a hard time when I'm playing with you guys.
It's hard playing with your best friends.

### • 339 •
The alarm on my watch went off during my backswing.

### • 340 •
I only par holes that I like.

## • 341 •

The dew on the green slowed up my putt.

## • 342 •

I forgot to take my vitamins this morning.
Now I'm out of energy.

## • 343 •

Your cell phone should have been turned off.

## • 344 •

I need yellow lenses for my sunglasses.
I'm getting too many ultraviolet rays.

### • 345 •

I thought this little shark on my shirt
would make me play better.

### • 346 •

I'm exhausted—the batteries in
my TV remote died yesterday.

### • 347 •

My thumb wasn't aligned with the club's axis.

### • 348 •

I never looked at the whole green.
It slopes left.

## • 349 •

The shade of that tree threw off my depth perception.

## • 350 •

I haven't been able to play since the car accident.
Too bad I can't sue for strokes.

## • 351 •

I'm too concerned about how my wife is playing
to worry about my own game.

## • 352 •

Your golf shirt is too bright.
Who the hell dresses you?

## • 353 •

I can't play unless I have sex prior to playing.

## • 354 •

I have sarcoidosis; I haven't been able to play.

## • 355 •

It's much windier on the West Coast.
I need at least thirty knots to play properly.

## • 356 •

I can't focus on golf when
my football team is playing.

My usual group is much better than you guys. They raise my level of play.

### • 358 •

I just can't envision the shot—
and that's the key to the whole game.

### • 359 •

I can only make the ten-footers;
the three-footers throw me off.

### • 360 •

The club only had small buckets available at the range.
I needed a large one.

### • 361 •

I teed the ball too low.

### • 362 •

I can't concentrate since I got fired.

### • 363 •

I've been preoccupied with the budget debate
going on in Congress.

### • 364 •

One of my shoelaces broke on the backswing.

### • 365 •

The sun dried out the green.
The balls are rolling too fast.

### • 366 •

Polo is my strong game.

### • 367 •

I never flared my left foot.

### • 368 •

I should have focused on the spot behind the ball.

### • 369 •

I was in Seattle the last three weeks
and all it did was rain. I couldn't practice.

### • 370 •

Since filing for bankruptcy, I can only golf twice a week.

### • 371 •

I thought the blue markers meant one hundred yards.

### • 372 •

This Alzheimer's makes me forget
where my ball landed.

### • 373 •

I only started playing again last month.

### • 374 •

I can't golf regularly for religious reasons.

### • 375 •

I thought cross-handed putting
was supposed to be the answer.

### • 376 •

I thought the white stake on the side
is what I was aiming for.
I didn't realize it was out-of-bounds.

### • 377 •

My body is swaying too much from the alcohol.

### • 378 •

I swung down too steeply on the ball.

### • 379 •

My feet must not have been parallel to the target.

### • 380 •

I moved my right knee on the backswing, creating an illusion of power that was improperly assessed.

### • 381 •

Since shooting sixty-eight,
I haven't been able to break one hundred.

### • 382 •

I can't afford golf lessons.

### • 383 •

My body tipped forward on the backswing, which
opened the face of the 3-wood, creating a slice.

### • 384 •

I was bent too far forward over the ball to get spin on it.

### • 385 •

The wind held the ball up in the air.
I knew I should have gone to services this morning.

## • 386 •

I feel guilty using tees made in China.

## • 387 •

My ball landed in a fairway divot because
some lazy butt didn't replace his.

## • 388 •

The greenkeeper aerated the fairways too early in the season.
I can't get any roll on the ball.

## • 389 •

I had my knees bent too far and I got way under the ball.

## • 390 •

The golf instruction videotape I bought
didn't teach me how to putt.

## • 391 •

The driving range wouldn't let me use
any of my woods, only irons.

## • 392 •

My putter shaft must be bent slightly.

## • 393 •

The water in the creek wasn't this high last week.
That would have been a great shot.

### • 394 •
I had a clump of mud on my ball,
causing it to go hard to the left.

### • 395 •
I'm getting old. I used to beat you all the time
when you were kids.

### • 396 •
The only tree on the entire hole...and I've hit it twice.

### • 397 •
My ball has a scuff on it from hitting the pin on
the last par 3. Now it spins too much around its axis.

### • 398 •

I haven't had time to practice my putting.

### • 399 •

On impact, my hips went through
too early and it opened up my swing,
causing the ball to angle improperly.

### • 400 •

I've only been golfing for a couple of years—
I don't have my swing down yet.

### • 401 •

This putter stinks. It has no lines on it to set up the putt.

## • 402 •

I need a beer and the cart girl hasn't been around.

## • 403 •

My short game is my strong suit, not driving.

## • 404 •

I never noticed this trap before.
I usually hit the green from 275 out.

## • 405 •

The wind blew sand in my eyes.

## • 406 •

I usually play with the club pro,
but he isn't here to give me tips.

## • 407 •

I put way too much spin on the ball
and it rolled off the green, down the hill,
bounced off that rake, and fell into the trap.

## • 408 •

I took too much of a divot and the ball came up short.

## • 409 •

I pulled my club too far back on the backswing,
creating insufficient torque on the forward transition.

## • 410 •

I only play well with forged clubs; cast clubs are too soft.

## • 411 •

I have a difficult time accepting a bad bounce
after hitting a great shot.

## • 412 •

I only read three angles to the putt.
I should have taken all four. I'm too lazy.

## • 413 •

It's so humid, I came out of the trap on the last hole
and the wind blew the sand in my face
and now it's stuck and I can't see.

**414**

The cart girl went home.
I can't relax.

## • 415 •

The ball just broke too much to the left.


## • 416 •

That leaf blew in front of my putt!


## • 417 •

I rotated my hands too far to the left, which made
the club face open at an improper point of the swing.


## • 418 •

The guy on the other green yelled right when
I was in my backswing.

### • 419 •

I aimed my shoulder too far left of the target.

### • 420 •

I have really bad jock itch
so my stance is all screwed up.

### • 421 •

I didn't flex my wrists on the backswing.

### • 422 •

I just don't play well in the sun, rain, clouds,
snow, or sleet—I lose my focus.

## • 423 •

I need new glasses.

## • 424 •

I was standing too close to the ball.

## • 425 •

My hair gel evaporated
and now my hair keeps getting in my eyes.

## • 426 •

I was kicked off my high school golf team.
I haven't played since. It's too emotionally painful.

### • 427 •

I just don't know what the hell I'm doing wrong.

### • 428 •

The golf seminar I wanted to go to was sold out.

### • 429 •

I can't get my mental checklist in its proper order.

### • 430 •

My dog ran away this morning,
so I didn't have time to warm up.

### • 431 •

I just choked...again.

### • 432 •

My calves hurt from running.

### • 433 •

I can only get enthusiastic about sex.
Golf just doesn't do it, so I don't try.

### • 434 •

My brother took my good golf glove.

### • 435 •

After that last shot, I'm just too embarrassed to try.

### • 436 •

The leaky faucet at home kept me up all night.

### • 437 •

I just can't get that triple bogey out of my head.

### • 438 •

I get so excited when I play that I can't relax.
I love this game!

## • 439 •
I am committed to my wife.
Golf has always come second.


## • 440 •
I am only out here to avoid my mother-in-law.


## • 441 •
My calculator must have run out of batteries.
Put me down for a three.


## • 442 •
I am constantly overestimating my ability.

### • 443 •
I played too much softball last week;
I'm hitting the ball too flat.

### • 444 •
I only care if I look good, not how I golf.

### • 445 •
I only took up the game to get away from the house.
I don't really care if I'm good.

### • 446 •
I only play for the camaraderie.

## • 447 •

I am so excited about
the World Series game tonight,
I can't focus.

## • 448 •

I knew I should have bought those rain gloves last week.

## • 449 •

My lucky argyles are in my other golf bag.
I can't putt without them.

## • 450 •

It hurts too much to practice, with the war injury and all.

### • 451 •

I can never get my last shot off my mind.

### • 452 •

My ex-girlfriend's brother-in-law is an old golf pro. He used to give me free golf lessons. If we had stayed together, I could have made that putt.

### • 453 •

I only play for personal, non-substantive goals.

### • 454 •

Golf isn't fun if it's competitive, so I don't try hard.

## • 455 •

The warden wouldn't let me practice
all those years in prison.

## • 456 •

I usually play the slice. Now I'm hitting it straight.
I just don't understand this game.

## • 457 •

The big mistake I always make is
expecting to play better than I do.
I have trouble handling disappointment.

## • 458 •

I thought the red stakes were a target toward the green.

### • 459 •

My cat chewed up my Thursday golf underwear.
I had to wear Sunday's.

### • 460 •

I'm not used to betting more than a quarter a hole.

### • 461 •

Some idiot ahead of us keeps
leaving sunflower seeds on the green.

### • 462 •

My mom used to iron all my socks.
I just can't get the crease the right way.

### • 463 •

I need one of those shark grips on my putter.
It seems to work for all the guys on the tour.

### • 464 •

I never even saw that tree next to the pond
next to the forest.

### • 465 •

I thought this was a par 6. I was just laying up.

### • 466 •

I thought you aim halfway when
chipping with a 9-iron.

### • 467 •

I don't care how I score when I'm young.
My only goal is to live long enough
to shoot lower than my age.

### • 468 •

I was surrounded by trees and did not have a shot.

### • 469 •

The ball broke to the right.
There must be a lake beyond that river.

### • 470 •

I have the yips; I just don't know what to do.

## • 471 •

It's cart-path only and I didn't have the right club.

## • 472 •

I can only chip with an 8-iron.
I must have left it on the last hole—
or maybe you are trying to sabotage my round.

## • 473 •

Bermuda grass sucks. My club keeps getting stuck.

## • 474 •

I usually hit the driver off the fairway fine.
The greenkeeper must be doing a poor job.

## • 475 •

I play for the exercise, not the score.

## • 476 •

I need to change my putting technique.

## • 477 •

I hit that well.
The golf gods must be against me today.

## • 478 •

I should have used the putter to get out of the bunker.

### • 479 •

My tempo is off since the incident with the ball washer.

### • 480 •

I dropped my left shoulder and hooked the ball.

### • 481 •

I can only get motivated to play golf
after watching *Caddyshack*.

### • 482 •

I'm used to playing in Alaska.
When I hit the pond, it's usually frozen. This isn't fair.

## • 483 •

I shot a seventy-one on this course last time.
Then again, it was on my computer.

## • 484 •

It was easier to putt when I wasn't good.
Now it's just too much pressure.

## • 485 •

My golf bag is too small.
I usually have a larger selection of clubs.

## • 486 •

These sneakers just don't give me
the proper support required for my ankles.

**487**

Golf is about etiquette, not about playing well.

## • 488 •

I'm used to playing courses with pine trees.
The oaks are distracting.

## • 489 •

I putted really well on the miniature golf course last night.

## • 490 •

I have two teenage daughters,
both of whom are going out tonight.
Need I say more?

## • 491•

The tee box has no grass in it.
I only play well at well-manicured courses.

**• 492•**

That duct tape just doesn't work as well as real grips.

**• 493 •**

I picked up my foot on my backswing.

**• 494 •**

I didn't come to play golf.
I wanted to see the Cubs in spring training.

**• 495 •**

What do you mean,
winter rules aren't allowed in the summer?

## • 496 •
I'm only playing for the charity.

## • 497 •
I'm gripping the club way too hard.

## • 498 •
I should have put more iron on the ball.

## • 499 •
I'm dehydrated from the heat.

## • 500 •

I'm used to playing night golf.
This daytime stuff confuses me.


## • 501 •

These clubs are instruments of torture—
I hate this game.

# ABOUT THE AUTHOR

. . . . . . . . . . . . . . . . . . . . . . .

Justin J. Exner is an airline executive with a BA in aviation business from Embry-Riddle Aeronautical University in Daytona Beach, Florida, and an MBA from Franklin University in Columbus, Ohio. He has played golf all over the world, and never makes a bad golf shot without a good reason. Justin golfs regularly and three-putts very frequently. He lives, works, and worships with his family in Haymarket, Virginia.